Kym

Congratulations
on your
Confirmation
Pentecost Sunday
19th May 2013
from
Reverend Pat Craighead
and
everyone at
St. Mary Magdalene
Longbenton

Jesus makes all things new!

REVELATION 21:5

Brownlow
GIFTS

Edited and compiled by
Paul C. Brownlow

ACKNOWLEDGMENTS

Every effort was made to properly attribute the sources of all quoted materials in this book. The quotes are not, in all cases, exact quotations as some have been edited for clarity and brevity, but in all cases, an attempt has been made to maintain the speaker's original intent. In some cases quoted material for the book was obtained from secondary sources, including print media and online websites. Although every effort was made to ensure the accuracy of the sources and attribution of the quotes, it cannot be guaranteed. We believe all materials (Bible references and quotations) contained herein are accurate, and we shall not be held liable for the same. If we have overlooked anything, please contact us. We will attempt to make any correction we deem necessary in future editions.

Grateful acknowledgment is made to the following:

http://www.christianquotes.org/
http://www.christiansquoting.org.uk/
http://www.great-quotes.com/
http://www.greatest-quotations.com/
http://www.iskandar.com/waleed911/motherteresa.html
http://www.litquotes.com/
http://www.motivationalquotes.com/
http://www.pietyhilldesign.com/gcq/index.html
http://www.quotesandsayings.com/
http://www.quotegarden.com/
http://www.quoteland.com/
http://www.quoteworld.org/
http://www.thinkexist.com/
http://www.worldofquotes.com/
http://www.zaadz.com/

*W*hy am I so depressed?
Why this turmoil within
me? Put your hope in God,
for I will still praise Him,
my Savior and my God.
Psalm 42:5 HCSB

*W*e must move from asking God to take care of the things that are breaking our hearts, to praying about the things that are breaking His heart.

Margaret Gibb

Lean on thyself until thy strength is tried; Then ask God's help; it will not be denied. Use thine own sight to see the way to go; When darkness falls, ask God the path to show.

Ella Wheeler Wilcox

I am always content with what happens; for I know that what God chooses is better than what I choose.
Epictetus

If you obey my commands, you will remain in my love,
just as I have obeyed my Father's commands and remain
in his love. I have told you this so that my joy may be
in you and that your joy may be complete.

John 15:10–11 NIV

....

....

....

....

....

....

....

....

....

....

....

....

....

....

God's promise to the pure of heart is of that knowledge of himself through love which is eternal life; and the heart will be pure when it is filled with the love of God "in all things and above all things." To be filled with such love is to have obtained the promises which exceed all that we can desire.

John Burnaby

Perhaps one reason God delays His answers to our prayers is because He knows we need to be with Him far more than we need the things we ask of Him.

Ben Patterson

We forget that God sometimes has to say "No". We pray to Him as our heavenly Father, and like wise human fathers, He often says, "No"– not from whim or caprice, but from wisdom and from love, and knowing what is best for us.

Peter Marshall

God is greater
than our hearts and
knows all things.
1 John 3:20 HCSB

When circumstances seem impossible, when all signs of grace in you seem at their lowest ebb, when temptation is fiercest, when love and joy and hope seem well-nigh extinguished in your heart, then rest, without feeling and without emotion, in the Father's faithfulness.

D. Tryon

God can make you
everything you want
to be, but you have to put
everything in his hands.
Mahalia Jackson

It will greatly comfort you if you can see God's hand in both your losses and your crosses.

Charles Haddon Spurgeon

*G*od is good. He is a refuge in times of trouble. He does care for us. But we must trust Him. We must replace fear with faith and self-pity with God-focused trust.

Robert J. Morgan

We wait in hope for the LORD; he is our help and our shield.

Psalm 33:20 NIV

We cannot abandon life because of its storms. The strongest trees are not found sheltered in the safety of the forest, rather they are in the open spaces—bent and twisted by winds of all seasons. God provides deep roots when there are wide-spreading branches.

Tammy Felton

He who trusts in himself is lost. He who trusts in God can do all things.

Alphonsus Liguori

"*For* I know the plans I have for you," declares the LORD, "plans to prosper you and not to harm you, plans to give you hope and a future."

Jeremiah 29:11 NIV

Were there no God, we would be in this glorious world with grateful hearts, and no one to thank.

Christina Rossetti

*W*hat other nation is so great as to have their gods near them the way the LORD our God is near us whenever we pray to him?

Deuteronomy 4:7 NIV

As I urged you, the moment you start praying, raise your heart upwards, and lower your eyes downwards; enter inside your inner person and pray in secret to your Father who is in heaven.

Aphrahat

There come times when I have nothing more to tell God. If I were to continue to pray in words, I would have to repeat what I have already said. At such times it is wonderful to say to God, "May I be in Thy presence, Lord? I have nothing more to say to Thee, but I do love to be in Thy presence."

Ole Hallesby

Snuggle in God's arms. When you are hurting, when you feel lonely, left out—let Him cradle you, comfort you, reassure you of His all-sufficient power and love.

Kay Arthur

*W*hatever you do in word or deed, do all in the name of the Lord Jesus, giving thanks to God the Father through Him.

Colossians 3:17 NKJV

Trust the past to God's
mercy, the present to
God's love, and the future
to God's providence.
Augustine

In those times when I can't seem to find God, I rest in the assurance that He knows how to find me.

Neva Coyle

God knows no distance.
Charleszetta Waddles

*L*ove the LORD your
God, listen to his voice,
and hold fast to him. For
the LORD is your life.
Deuteronomy 30:20 NIV

God will not permit any troubles to come upon us, unless He has a specific plan by which great blessing can come out of the difficulty.

Peter Marshall

The LORD is good, a refuge in times of trouble.
He cares for those who trust in Him.

Nahum 1:7 NIV

*A*re you facing fear today? Don't allow fear
to keep you from being used by God. He has kept
you thus far; trust Him for the rest of the way.

Woodrow Kroll

We are to give our heart to God that he may make it happy, with a happiness which stretches its capacity to the full.

Gordon S. Wakefield

*W*hat you need to do, is to put your will over completely into the hands of your Lord, surrendering to Him the entire control of it. Say, "Yes, Lord, YES!" to everything, and trust Him to work in you to will, as to bring your whole wishes and affections into conformity with His own sweet, and lovable, and most lovely will. It is wonderful what miracles God works in wills that are utterly surrendered to Him. He turns hard things into easy, and bitter things into sweet. It is not that He puts easy things in the place of the hard, but He actually changes the hard thing into an easy one.

Hannah Whitall Smith

We can walk without fear, full of hope and courage and strength to do His will, waiting for the endless good which He is always giving as fast as He can get us able to take it in.

George MacDonald

When they call on me, I will answer; I will be with them in trouble. I will rescue them and honor them.

Psalm 91:15 NLT

Trust God for great things; with your five loaves and two fishes, he will show you a way to feed thousands.
Horace Bushnell

See in the meantime that your faith brings forth obedience, and God in due time will cause it to bring forth peace.

John Owen

Faith, mighty faith, the promise sees, And looks to God alone;
Laughs at impossibilities, And cries it shall be done.

Charles Wesley

Now this is the confidence that we have in Him, that if we ask anything according to His will, He hears us.
1 John 5:14 NKJV

*God's way of answering the Christian's prayer
for more patience, experience, hope and love often
is to put him into the furnace of affliction.*
Richard Cecil

Trust in the Lord with all your heart, and do not rely on your own understanding; think about Him in all your ways, and He will guide you on the right paths.

Proverbs 3:5-6 HCSB

*M*ay the Lord of peace Himself give you peace always in every way.

2 Thessalonians 3:16 HCSB

You must live with people to know their problems, and live with God in order to solve them.

Peter Taylor Forsyth

Trust in Him at all times, you people; Pour out your heart before Him; God is a refuge for us.

Psalm 62:8 NKJV

But when you pray, go
into your private room,
shut your door, and pray to
your Father who is in secret.
And your Father who sees
in secret will reward you.
Matthew 6:6 HCSB

Those who trust in the Lord will find new strength. They will soar high on wings like eagles. They will run and not grow weary. They will walk and not faint.

Isaiah 40:31 NLT

The peace of God is that eternal calm which lies far too deep in the praying, trusting soul to be reached by any external disturbances.

Arthur Tappan Pierson

I have had prayers answered—most strangely sometimes—
but I think our heavenly Father's loving kindness has
been even more evident in what He has refused me.

Lewis Carroll

If you abide in Me, and
My words abide in you, you
will ask what you desire, and
it shall be done for you.
John 15:7 NKJV

God delights in our
temptations and yet hates
them. He delights in them
when they drive us to prayer;
He hates them when they
drive us to despair.

Martin Luther

I will call upon the LORD, who is worthy to be praised; So shall I be saved from my enemies.

Psalm 18:3 NKJV

The acid test of our faith in the promises of God is never found in the easy-going, comfortable ways of life, but in the great emergencies, the times of storm and of stress, the days of adversity, when all human aid fails.

Ethel Bell

The more we depend on God, the more dependable we find he is.
Cliff Richard

How often we look upon God as our last and feeblest resource! We go to Him because we have nowhere else to go. And then we learn that the storms of life have driven us, not upon the rocks, but into the desired haven.

George MacDonald

*M*any believe—and I believe—that I have been designated for this work by God. In spite of my old age, I do not want to give it up; I work out of love for God and I put all my hope in Him.

Michelangelo

Faith will turn any course, light any path, relieve any distress, bring joy out of sorrow, peace out of strife, friendship out of enmity, heaven out of hell. Faith is God at work.

F. L. Holmes

Don't worry about anything; instead, pray about everything. Tell God what you need, and thank him for all he has done.

Philippians 4:6 NLT

The ultimate ground
of faith and knowledge
is confidence in God.

Charles Hodge

Again I say to you that if two of you agree
on earth concerning anything that they ask, it will
be done for them by My Father in heaven.

Matthew 18:19 NKJV

*S*ince God knows our future, our personalities, and our capacity to listen, He isn't ever going to say more to us than we can deal with at the moment.

Charles Stanley

*Blessed is the man who
trusts in the Lord, and
whose hope is the Lord.*
Jeremiah 17:7 NKJV

In prayer we can find reassurance, for God will speak peace to the soul. That peace, that spirit of serenity, is life's greatest blessing.

Ezra Taft Benson

*Darkness cannot put out the Light.
It can only make God brighter.*

Unknown

On days when life is difficult and I feel overwhelmed, as I do fairly often, it helps to remember in my prayers that all God requires of me is to trust Him and be His friend. I find I can do that.

Bruce Larson

Leave it with the Lord, and remember that what you trust to Him you must not worry over nor feel anxious about.
Hannah Whitall Smith

*M*y prayer today is that
we will feel the loving arms
of God wrapped around us,
and will know in our hearts
that He will never forsake
us as we trust in Him.

Billy Graham

Be of good courage, And He shall strengthen
your heart, All you who hope in the LORD.
Psalm 31:24 NKJV

*When all else is gone,
God is left, and nothing
changes Him.*
Hannah Whitall Smith

When you suffer and
lose, that does not mean
you are being disobedient
to God. In fact, it might
mean you're right in
the center of His will.
The path of obedience
is often marked by times
of suffering and loss.

Charles Swindoll

*C*ast yourself into the arms of God and be very sure that if He wants anything of you, He will fit you for the work and give you strength.

Philip Neri

Lift up your eyes. The heavenly Father waits to
bless you in inconceivable ways to make your life
what you never dreamed it could be.

Anne Ortlund

For God so loved the world that he gave his
one and only Son, that whoever believes in him
shall not perish but have eternal life.
John 3:16 NIV

God will not look you over for medals, degrees, or diplomas, but for scars.

Elbert Hubbard

*W*e are children of God;
and it has not yet been
revealed what we shall be,
but we know that when He
is revealed, we shall be like
Him, for we shall see Him
as He is. And everyone who
has this hope in Him purifies
himself, just as He is pure.

1 John 3:2–3 NKJV

It is impossible to have the feeling of peace
and serenity without being at rest with God.

Dorothy Pentecost

*M*irth is God's medicine. Everybody ought to bathe in it. Grim care, moroseness, anxiety —all this rust of life ought to be scoured off by the oil of mirth.

Henry Ward Beecher

It is pleasing to God
whenever thou rejoicest
or laughest from the
bottom of thy heart.
Martin Luther

The path of duty is the only path of safety. It is the only path wherein we can walk and have the assurance of God's continued blessings, of his continued deliverances.

George Reynolds

The LORD has done great things for us,
and we are filled with joy.
Psalm 126:3 NIV

*Keep praying, but be thankful that God's answers
are wiser than your prayers.*

William Culbertson

*L*et me experience
Your faithful love in the
morning, for I trust in You.
Psalm 143:8 HCSB

The Bible is meant to be bread for our daily use, not just cake for special occasions.
Anonymous

The moment He imagined creation He imagined the end. It's the future that's informing your present. God knows what the next chapter is and so He's pouring into the present.
Reggie McNeal

Start living now. Stop saving the good china for that special occasion. Stop withholding your love until that special person materializes. Every day you are alive is a special occasion. Every minute, every breath, is a gift from God.

Mary Manin Morrissey

Jesus commands us to "watch and pray." If we are able to be persons of faith, then we will be persons of prayer. If we are to be persons of hope and healing in the world, then we will be persons for whom living is praying, and praying is living. In short, we have no choice but to pray.

Conrad Hoover

*The Lord is a faithful God. Blessed are
those who wait for his help.*

Isaiah 30:18 NLT

Therefore, since we have been declared righteous by faith, we have peace with God through our Lord Jesus Christ. Also through Him, we have obtained access by faith into this grace in which we stand.

Romans 5:1,2 HCSB

Father, hear the prayer we offer; not for ease that prayer shall be, but for strength that we may ever live our lives courageously.

Maria Willis

If you have been mistreated, cheated or deceived and if your heart has been right all along, be assured that God knows this. God will eventually vindicate you, but in the meantime you should be confidently aware that God knows the truth concerning what has happened to you. He knows if your heart has been right.

Theodore Epp

When you are praying,
first forgive anyone you are
holding a grudge against, so
that your Father in heaven
will forgive your sins, too.
Mark 11:25 NLT

God's gifts put man's best dreams to shame.
Elizabeth Barrett Browning

It is impossible for that man
to despair who remembers
that his helper is omnipotent.
Jeremy Taylor

Thus says the LORD, the
God of David your father:
"I have heard your prayer,
I have seen your tears;
surely I will heal you."
2 Kings 20:5 NKJV

Two men please God—who serves Him with all his heart because he knows Him; who seeks Him with all his heart because he knows Him not.

Nikita Ivanovich Panin

God does not comfort us to make us
comfortable, but to make us comforters.

John Henry Jowett

In life, if we have hope in God, it makes us happy. Jesus is all that we need.

Dorothy Thompson

Everything we call a trial, a sorrow or a duty, believe me, that angel's hand is there, the gift is there, and the wonder of an overshadowing presence. Our joys, too, be not content with them as joys. They, too, conceal diviner gifts.

Fra Giovanni Giocondo

The will of God is never exactly what you expect it to be. It may seem to be much worse, but in the end it's going to be a lot better and a lot bigger.

Elisabeth Elliot

As a mother comforts her child, so will I
comfort you; and you will be comforted.

Isaiah 66:13 NIV

There are some favors the Almighty does not grant either the first, or the second, or the third time you ask him, because he wishes you to pray for a long time and often. He wills this delay to keep you in a state of humility and self-contempt and make you realize the value of his graces.

John Eudes

Life without God, to one who has known the richness and joy of life with Him, is unthinkable, impossible.

Phillips Brooks

The blessing of the Lord makes a person rich.

Proverbs 10:22 NLT

Does your need seem big to you? Then make sure that God knows how big it looks to your eyes and He will treat it as such. He will never belittle it however trivial. He will not laugh at it, or at us. He never forgets how large our problems look to us.

Corrie ten Boom

With a strong affirmation of our goodness
and a gentle understanding of our weakness, God
is loving us—you and me—this moment, just
as we are and not as we should be.

Brennan Manning

The LORD will give
strength to His people;
The LORD will bless
His people with peace.

Psalm 29:11 NKJV

*P*eace is the gift of God. Do you want peace? Go to God.

John Taylor

We need not fear life, because God is the Ruler of all and we need not fear death, because He shares immortality with us.

Ann Landers

The degree of blessing
enjoyed by any man will
correspond exactly with
the completeness of
God's victory over him.

A.W. Tozer

To be at one with God is to be at peace . . . peace is to be found only within, and unless one finds it there he will never find it at all. Peace lies not in the external world. It lies within one's own soul.

Ralph W. Trine

I will trust Him. Whatever, wherever I am, I can never be thrown away. If I am in sickness, my sickness may serve Him; in perplexity, my perplexity may serve Him; if I am in sorrow, my sorrow may serve Him. My sickness, or perplexity, or sorrow may be necessary causes of some great end, which is quite beyond us. He does nothing in vain.

John Henry Newman

God is our refuge and strength,
an ever-present help in trouble.
Psalm 46:1 NIV

I pray and meditate every single day, every morning. You know, I pray in cabs. I pray in airplanes. I don't really ask for anything I just pray that Jesus will give me the strength to follow Him. That's all I pray for. And that I will always turn my will and my life over to His care.

Lawrence Kudlow

You are confronted again and again with the choice of letting God speak or letting your wounded self cry out. Although there has to be a place where you can allow your wounded part to get the attention it needs, your vocation is to speak from the place in you where God dwells.

Henri J. M. Nouwen

It is not worrying, but rather trusting and abiding in the peace of God that will crush anything that Satan tries to do to us. If the Lord created the world out of chaos, He can easily deal with any problem that we have.

Rick Joyner

Our responsibility is to keep knocking at God's door . . . to keep believing God will answer our prayers. . . . Patiently but expectantly wait on the Lord.

Thelma Wells

*Humble yourselves,
therefore, under God's
mighty hand, that he may
lift you up in due time.
Cast all your anxiety on him
because he cares for you.*
1 Peter 5:6–7 NIV

In almost everything that touches our everyday life on earth, God is pleased when we're pleased. He wills that we be as free as birds to soar and sing our Maker's praise without anxiety.

A. W. Tozer

If the Lord be with us, we have no cause of fear.
His eye is upon us, His arm over us, His ear open to our
prayer—His grace sufficient, His promises unchangeable.

John Newton

Faith is not believing that God can, it is knowing that He will.
Unknown

Just as there comes a warm sunbeam into every cottage window, so comes a love-beam of God's care and pity for every separate need.

Nathaniel Hawthorne

Cast your burden on the Lord, and He will support you; He will never allow the righteous to be shaken.

Psalm 55:22 HCSB

Faith is deliberate confidence in the character of God whose ways you may not understand at the time.

Oswald Chambers

God doesn't always answer in the way we like or in ways we can fathom, but I believe God knows us and notices us and is willing to invest and involve himself in our lives.

Timothy Jones

Jesus answered and said to them, "Have faith in God. For assuredly, I say to you, whoever says to this mountain, 'Be removed and be cast into the sea,' and does not doubt in his heart, but believes that those things he says will be done, he will have whatever he says."

Mark 11:22–23 NKJV

When God is involved, anything can happen. Be open. Stay that way. God has a beautiful way of bringing good vibrations out of broken chords.

Charles Swindoll

Light shines on the godly, and joy on those whose hearts are right.
Psalm 97:11 NLT

*W*hen we let God's Word seep into our own lives little by little...
it nourishes us and becomes part of us.

Janette Oke

God will wipe away every tear from their eyes; there shall be no more death, nor sorrow, nor crying. There shall be no more pain, for the former things have passed away.

Revelation 21:4 NKJV

When you and I hurt deeply,
what we really need is not
an explanation from God
but a revelation of God. We
need to see how great God is;
we need to recover our lost
perspective on life. Things
get out of proportion when
we are suffering, and it takes
a vision of something bigger
than ourselves to get life's
dimensions adjusted again.

Warren W. Wiersbe

The LORD's delight is
in those who honor him,
those who put their hope
in his unfailing love.
Psalm 147:11 NLT

The world is crooked and God straightens it.
Alexander Elchaninov

What a joy and peace comes to our hearts when we learn to give those situations to the Lord, to commit them to Him, to entrust them to the One who can do the impossible.

Robert J. Morgan

Let nothing disturb me.
Let nothing frighten me.
Let nothing take away
my peace. May I wait
with trust, with patience,
knowing you will provide
for me. I lack for nothing
in You, God. You are my
strong foundation. You are
enough for me.

Teresa of Avila

Finally, brothers, rejoice. Be restored, be encouraged, be of the same mind, be at peace, and the God of love and peace will be with you.
2 Corinthians 13:11 HCSB

God brings men into deep waters, not to drown
them, but to cleanse them.
John H. Aughey

Trials should not surprise us, or cause us to doubt God's faithfulness. Rather, we should actually be glad for them. God sends trials to strengthen our trust in him so that our faith will not fail. Our trials keep us trusting; they burn away our self-confidence and drive us to our Savior.

Edmund Clowney

*O*ur God can handle even the worst that can happen to us as finite human beings. Since Christ is beside us, no troubles that life can bring need cast us adrift. This is a knowledge which can release us from lifelong bondage to fear.

Catherine Marshall

Hope is the word which God has written on the brow of every man.

Victor Hugo

*Y*ou know that the LORD your God is the only true God. So love him and obey his commands, and he will faithfully keep his agreement with you and your descendants for a thousand generations.

Deuteronomy 7:9 CEV

God knows best; he hasn't arranged your anatomy so as to make it easy for you to pat yourself on the back.

Unknown

Circumstances may appear to wreck our lives and God's plans, but God is not helpless among the ruins. God's love is still working. He comes in and takes the calamity and uses it victoriously, working out His wonderful plan of love.
Eric Liddell

God is not nearly as concerned with our getting
what we want as He is with our getting him.

George Myers

The best remedy for those who are afraid, lonely or unhappy is to go outside, somewhere where they can be quiet, alone with the heavens, nature and God. Because only then does one feel that all is as it should be.

Anne Frank

"For I will restore health to you and heal you of your wounds," says the LORD.
Jeremiah 30:17 NKJV

*L*ook to your health; and if you have it, praise God and value it next to conscience; for health is the second blessing that we mortals are capable of, a blessing money can't buy.

Izaak Walton

Blessings are only signs of God's love. The real blessing, of course, is the love itself.
Craig Barnes

Should we feel at times disheartened and discouraged,
a confiding thought, a simple movement of heart towards God will
renew our powers. Whatever He may demand of us, He will give us
at the moment the strength and the courage that we need.

François de la Fénelon

If you have been
reduced to God being
your only hope, you
are in a good place.

Jim Laffoon

*H*ope in God;
For I shall yet praise
Him, the help of my
countenance and
my God.
Psalm 42:11 NKJV

In the secret of God's tabernacle no enemy can find us, and no troubles can reach us. The pride of man and the strife of tongues find no entrance into the pavilion of God. The secret of his presence is a more secure refuge than a thousand Gibraltars. I do not mean that no trials come. They may come in abundance, but they cannot penetrate into the sanctuary of the soul, and we may dwell in perfect peace even in the midst of life's fiercest storms.

Hannah Whitall Smith

Each of us has a capacity for God and an ability to relate to him in a personal way. When we do, he brings to us pardon for the past, peace for the present, and a promise for the future.

Ralph Bell

In His wisdom God does not show us all that lies ahead. So we enter a new year to live it day by day. What is past is past. Today we start anew, and what we do today will make our life for tomorrow. Each day let us follow more faithfully, more courageously, more daringly the lead of our great Captain who bids us follow Him.

William Thomson Hanzsche

Thank God every morning when you get up that you have something to do that day which must be done, whether you like it or not.

Charles Kingsley

We are commanded to love God with all our minds, as well as with all our hearts, and we commit a great sin if we forbid or prevent that cultivation of the mind in others which would enable them to perform this duty.

Angelina Grimke

How blessed and amazing are God's gifts, dear friends! Life with immortality, splendor with righteousness, truth with confidence, faith with assurance, self-control with holiness! And all these things are within our comprehension.

Clement of Rome

Consider the lilies, how they grow: they neither toil nor spin; and yet I say to you, even Solomon in all his glory was not arrayed like one of these. If then God so clothes the grass, which today is in the field and tomorrow is thrown into the oven, how much more will He clothe you, O you of little faith?

Luke 12:27–28 NKJV

Man finds it hard to get what he wants, because he does not want the best; God finds it hard to give, because He would give the best, and man will not take it.

George MacDonald

Be assured, if you walk with Him, and look to Him,
and expect help from Him, He will never fail you.

George Mueller

It appears that when life is broken by tragedy,
God shines through the breach.

George A. Buttrick

When we go through trials and troubles we can always rely on God and know that He will be with us and will help us through. Clouds and rain can help make your roots strong and give you stability if you let God work through them. So let us rejoice in our clouds and rain and know that God is still in control even when we can't see Him.

David Vincent, in *Living with Muscular Dystrophy*

I will both lie down and sleep in peace, for You alone, LORD, make me live in safety.

Psalm 4:8 HCSB

There may be those on earth who dress better or eat better, but those who enjoy the peace of God sleep better.

L. Thomas Holdcroft

It is in the deepest darkness of the starless midnight
that men learn how to hold on to the hidden Hand most
tightly and how that Hand holds them; that He sees where
we do not, and knows the way He takes; and though the
way be to us a roundabout way, it is the right way.

Arthur Tappan Pierson

Our circumstances are
not an accurate reflection
of God's goodness.
Whether life is good or bad,
God's goodness, rooted in
His character, is the same.
Helen Grace Lescheid

And even in our sleep,
pain that cannot forget
falls drop by drop upon
the heart, and in our own
despair, against our will,
comes wisdom to us by the
grace of God.

Aeschylus

*P*eace comes when there is no cloud between us and God. Peace is the consequence of forgiveness, God's removal of that which obscures His face and so breaks union with Him. The happy sequence culminating in fellowship with God is penitence, pardon, and peace—the first we offer, the second we accept, and the third we inherit.

Charles H. Brent

When all our efforts have come to nothing, we naturally tend to doubt not just ourselves, but also whether God is just. At those moments, our only hope is to seek every evidence that God is just, by communing with the people we know who are strongest in faith.

Bill Moyers

The soul can split the sky in two and
let the face of God shine through.

Edna St. Vincent Millay

*B*lessed is a man who
endures trials, because
when he passes the test he
will receive the crown of
life that God has promised
to those who love Him.

James 1:12 HCSB

I believe in the sun even if it isn't shining. I believe in love even when I am alone. I believe in God even when He is silent.

Found on a cellar wall in Cologne, Germany where Jews hid during World War II

Watch, stand fast in the faith, be brave, be strong.

1 Corinthians 16:13 NKJV

God sometimes shuts
the door and shuts us
in, that He may speak,
perchance through grief or
pain, and softly, heart to
heart, above the din, may
tell some precious thought
to us again.

Unknown

Each of us may be sure
that if God sends us on
stony paths He will provide
us with strong shoes, and
He will not send us out on
any journey for which He
does not equip us well.
Alexander MacLaren

And now, Lord, for what do I wait? My hope is in You.

Psalm 39:7 NASV

There is a deep peace that grows out of illness and loneliness and a sense of failure. God cannot get close when everything is delightful. He seems to need these darker hours, these empty-hearted hours, to mean the most to people.

Frank C. Laubach

God of our life, there are days when the burdens we carry chafe our shoulders and weigh us down; when the road seems dreary and endless, the skies grey and threatening; when our lives have no music in them, and our hearts are lonely, and our souls have lost their courage. Flood the path with light, run our eyes to where the skies are full of promise; tune our hearts to brave music; give us the sense of comradeship with heroes and saints of every age; and so quicken our spirits that we may be able to encourage the souls of all who journey with us on the road of life, to Your honor and glory.

Augustine

Through the LORD's mercies we are not consumed, Because His compassions fail not. They are new every morning; Great is Your faithfulness.

Lamentations 3:22–23 NKJV

Before me, even as behind, God is, and all is well.

John Greenleaf Whittier

If you feel like you're at the end of your rope,
tie a knot and hang on! Because God's a God of
miracles, and He's holding the other end.

Pat Hicks

Do you need help today? Lift up your hands to the Lord in supplication and in expectation, and soon you will lift up your hands in jubilation and celebration.

Warren W. Wiersbe

He comes to us in the brokenness of our health, in the shipwreck of our family lives, in the loss of all possible peace of mind, even in the very thick of our sins. He saves us in our disasters, not from them. He emphatically does not promise to meet only the odd winner of the self-improvement lottery: He meets us all in our endless and inescapable losing.

Robert Farrar Capon

Every morning is a fresh opportunity to find God's extraordinary joy in the most ordinary places.

Janet L. Weaver

The LORD is my light and my salvation; Whom shall I fear? The LORD is the strength of my life; Of whom shall I be afraid?

Psalm 27:1 NKJV

God has an especial tenderness of love towards thee for that thou art in the dark and hast no light . . . For he sees thee through all the gloom through which thou canst not see Him.

George MacDonald

You love Him, though you have not seen Him. And though not seeing Him now, you believe in Him and rejoice with inexpressible and glorious joy, because you are receiving the goal of your faith, the salvation of your souls.

1 Peter 1:8,9 HCSB

If the Spirit of God detects anything in you that is wrong, He does not ask you to put it right; He asks you to accept the light, and He will put it right.

Oswald Chambers

We get new ideas from God every hour of our day when we put our trust in Him—but we have to follow that inspiration up with perspiration—we have to work to prove our faith. Remember that the bee that hangs around the hive never gets any honey.

Albert E. Cliffe

God does not give us everything we want, but he does fulfill his promises . . . leading us along the best and straightest paths to himself.

Dietrich Bonhoeffer

He would grant you, according to the riches of His glory, to be strengthened with might through His Spirit in the inner man, that Christ may dwell in your hearts through faith.

Ephesians 3:16–17 NKJV

God has not promised
an easy way, but peace at
the center of the hard way.
Dale Evans Rogers